W9-CGS-209

The Divorce Resource Series

Understanding the Law

A Teen Guide to Family Court and Minors' Rights

CHAVEZ HIGH SCHOOL
LIBRARY
HOUSTON, TEXAS

Anne Bianchi

THE ROSEN PUBLISHING GROUP, INC.
NEW YORK

Published in 2000 by The Rosen Publishing Group, Inc.
29 East 21st Street, New York, NY 10010

Copyright © 2000 by The Rosen Publishing Group, Inc.

First Edition

All rights reserved. No part of this book may be reproduced in any form without permission in writing from the publisher, except by a reviewer.

Cataloging-in-Publication Data

Bianchi, Anne, 1948-
    Understanding the law: a teen guide to family court and minors' rights/ Anne Bianchi.
        p. cm.— (The divorce resource series)
    Includes bibliographical references and index.
    Summary: This book explains the legal process of divorce, including custody of children, alimony, child support, and the division of property, and discusses the role of a court of law in divorce cases.
    ISBN 0-8239-3152-8
    1. Divorce— Law and legislation— United States— Juvenile literature. 2. Divorce settlements— United States— Juvenile literature. 3. Custody of children— United States— Juvenile literature. [1. Divorce   2. Custody of children] I. Title. II. Series.
    346.7301'66— dc21

Manufactured in the United States of America

Contents

CHAPTER 1

What Is a Divorce?

What is a divorce? A divorce is the legal termination, or end, of a marriage. The word "legal" is important here for many reasons. It implies that courts of law, judges, and lawyers are all involved in a divorce. It implies that a divorce is a kind of legal agreement, which means that it is legally binding and can be legally enforced. In other words, the parties to the divorce—the man and woman who no longer wish to be married to each other—agree to certain conditions under which their marriage will be legally ended.

The most important of those conditions involve the division of property that belongs to the couple and, when the couple have children, what is known as custody.

You may go to court for your parents' divorce.

Most often, property refers to the house or apartment the family lived in. Property can also include furniture, cars, and, in some places, money—savings and investments, including stocks and bonds and other financial instruments.

Custody refers to which parent will have the primary legal right and responsibility of raising the children. To say that this agreement is legally binding and can be legally enforced means that either party to the agreement—the former husband or the former wife—can use the legal system to make certain that the other party does what he or she has agreed to do.

For example, a common situation in a divorce settlement is that the former husband agrees to pay alimony to his former wife and, if she receives custody of their children, child support. Alimony is an amount of money, or an allowance, paid by one spouse to the other for support after a divorce. The most common scenario is that the former husband pays his ex-wife alimony, although it does happen the other way around in a small number of cases. Child support is money paid by one of the parents to the parent with custody for the expenses of raising and caring for their children—food, clothing, and education, at minimum. If the person who is supposed to pay alimony and child support does not do so, the other party to the divorce can go to court to have their agreement enforced.

However, to say that the couple in a divorce proceeding agree to the legal terms under which the divorce is to occur is somewhat misleading. Anyone who is remotely familiar with divorce—even if it is just from reading about sensational cases in the newspaper, such as the high-profile breakup of cosmetics mogul Ron Perelman and socialite Patricia Duff that dominated tabloid headlines throughout 1999—knows that a divorce can be the most bitter of disagreements.

Duff and Perelman, for example, had resources that should have made it easier for them to agree on the terms of their divorce—resources that the vast majority of families will never enjoy. For many of the families fortunate enough to own the house or apartment in which they live, for example—and in the United States, almost 40 percent of households do not—their home is the largest single investment they will ever make and the largest financial asset they will ever have. When you add the strength of emotional attachments and the natural concern of parents for how their children will live, you can understand how a house could become an issue in a divorce settlement.

For many of the same reasons, it is easy to understand why issues of child custody and support can be so hard to resolve for many families. Similarly, for most families that go through a divorce, financial questions

are a much more critical issue than they were for Perelman and Duff. Generally speaking, married women in the United States live at a higher economic level than single or divorced women, even when one adjusts for such factors as education, career achievement, and the socioeconomic level of the family into which they were born. When a woman, either with or without children, slips from above to below poverty level in the United States, the most common factor is divorce or abandonment by her husband.

None of these concerns applied to Duff and Perelman. In late 1999, the custody portion of their divorce suit was in its fourth year, which made it almost as old as their daughter. The marriage itself had lasted just twenty months. Perelman was Duff's fourth husband; she was his fourth wife. Before the marriage, Perelman's net worth was estimated at $4.2 billion and he owned three lavish homes.

Duff was much less wealthy on her own, but she was still much better off than most women who face divorce. The prenuptial agreement she had signed with Perelman left Duff with a net worth estimated at $30 million, including about $5 million in cash, jewelry valued at $4.5 million, two houses in Connecticut estimated to be worth $6 million, and antiques and art appraised at a total worth of $7.5 million. (A prenuptial agreement is a contract

Ron Perelman's divorce was highly publicized.

signed before a wedding in which the couple agree on what the financial terms will be if the marriage ends.) In addition, Duff was to receive an allowance of $1.2 million each year until she remarried or her daughter was of age.

Clearly, financial well-being and worries about whether their daughter would have a roof over her head were not issues for Duff and Perelman. Still, the two found reasons to disagree. The dispute centered on child-care provisions. While living with her daughter in a $30,000-a-month suite in the luxurious Waldorf-Astoria Hotel in New York City, Duff asked her former husband for $60,000 per month in temporary child support. On a more permanent basis, Duff wanted $267,000 for her daughter each month. This included, *each month*, $15,000 for vacations, $21,000 for household help, $1,750 in beauty parlor treatments, $15,000 for clothing for herself, and $3,000 for her daughter. By the end of 1999, with the dispute still unsettled, Duff was using her sixteenth different law firm in the case, and each party had spent hundreds of thousands of dollars in legal fees.

Many of those who read about Perelman and Duff's court battle found it hard to believe. How could two people who had been so fortunate, in terms of financial success, find anything to argue about with regard to the support of their daughter?

Surely there was enough money to make sure the girl was well taken care of.

The point to be understood with regard to Duff and Perelman's troubles is that when couples argue about financial and property matters in a divorce, they are not always arguing only about money. Sometimes money, property, and child-custody issues are the ways by which a divorcing couple try to settle the hurt and unresolved emotional issues from the marriage. They become means of settling the score or getting even instead of determining the best and fairest way for the family to continue after the divorce.

Do all divorce cases become as destructive as the one between Perelman and Duff? No. Just as that case is unusual in the amount of money involved, it is special in the length and intensity of the legal battle. But when the parties to a divorce cannot reach an agreement on any of the necessary issues, then a court of law will make that agreement for them, as the court is trying to do in the Duff-Perelman case. How and why a court does that is the subject of this book.

CHAPTER 2

Why Should the Courts Be Involved?

When Caitlin's parents told her and her younger sister, Allison, that they were going to divorce, Caitlin couldn't say that she was either shocked or disappointed. Her actual feelings surprised her. She felt relieved, even a little bit glad.

Caitlin's parents argued, but not a lot. She had heard a lot worse, and much more often, at some of her friends' houses. Her parents went to a great deal of trouble not to argue in front of her and Allison. Even when they were upset with each other, they didn't shout and scream, insult each other, or call each other names, which was something she had actually heard in other homes. When she told her friend Jackie that her parents were splitting up, Jackie actually asked her if her dad ever hit her mom or if her mom threw things. Caitlin

Your friends may be concerned and want to ask you questions about your parents divorce.

almost laughed out loud. The thought of her parents behaving that way was quite funny, even preposterous.

Her parents liked each other, that was the thing. They laughed a lot together, talked a lot, and counted on each other in a lot of ways. As a mother and a father, they were tremendous. Even Caitlin's friends were always telling her how great her parents were. It seemed that there were always other kids in the house, and they were always made to feel welcome. Any time that Caitlin's mom and dad had outside of work, they gave to their children. The two girls knew that their parents were always available for them.

Caitlin had to admit that she and Allison had just about everything they wanted, and even more than they actually needed. Some of the other kids lived in houses that were bigger and nicer, but Allison didn't think that those homes were necessarily any happier. She was old enough to understand things like that now.

She was also old enough to think about and understand other things, too, stuff that maybe Allison couldn't yet. Although her parents rarely seemed to be angry with each other, Caitlin doubted that they were happy. They didn't sleep in the same room, let alone the same bed. They never kissed or touched each other, not even for an affectionate hug.

When Caitlin told her friend Tamara that her parents were getting a divorce, Tamara said that probably her dad had a new girlfriend or her mom had a boyfriend. But Caitlin didn't think that was the case, either. She knew such things were possible, of course, but she just didn't think that was what was happening in her family. For one thing, she couldn't imagine when either of her parents would have the time to see someone else. They were always either working or at home taking care of her and Allison.

Caitlin just figured that her parents needed something a little different. She believed them when they said that they still cared very deeply for each other and that they would still take the same kind of good care of her and Allison. She was sad that the whole family would not be living in the same house together anymore, but she was actually kind of glad for her parents. Things were often a little tense in the house, and maybe her parents could actually be happy now, instead of just dutiful and responsible. The whole thing was probably harder for Allison because she was younger, but Caitlin could help her sister with that.

Even so, Caitlin did have a bunch of questions. How do people actually get a divorce anyway? People who get divorced have to go to court, don't they? Would some judge be telling her family how to live from now on? Would she and Allison have to answer a lot of questions from strangers? Why was what went on in her family anybody else's business anyway?

A Legal Issue?

What Caitlin most wanted to know was this: Why did a court, and lawyers and judges and everything that goes with it, have to be involved at all? Why should divorce be a legal issue, instead of just an emotional issue? Why was it anyone's business, besides the members of her family, that her parents were getting divorced?

Marriage: More Than a Matter of the Heart

The idea that marriage is a legal issue can be a difficult, even shocking, thing for many people to understand. Indeed, for many people, the first true understanding of this fact comes when they become involved in a divorce. After all, this society celebrates marriage as the ultimate romantic experience, the climax of a fairy tale in which husband and wife supposedly live "happily ever after." Marriage is supposed to be permanent, or to last forever, "until death do us part," in the words of some marriage vows. This is why the idea of a prenuptial agreement is so upsetting to some people. It introduces an unwelcome aspect of reality or practicality to what many people would prefer to think of only as a romantic ideal.

Even so, marriage is a legal arrangement as much as a moral, religious, emotional, or romantic one. Many people

The idea that marriage is a legal issue can be a difficult thing for people to understand.

get married in a religious ceremony conducted by a member of the clergy, but in the United States that marriage still needs to be registered legally. That is why people have to apply for a marriage license even if they are married in a church, synagogue, or other house of worship.

The question then becomes why this should be so. Laws and the legal system are the means that society, as represented by the government, uses to regulate, or control, aspects of life in which it takes an interest. In a democratic society such as the United States, however, it is understood that there are certain aspects of individual behavior that the government cannot legitimately attempt to control. Examples of such areas include what a person says, what religion a person practices, what organizations a person belongs to, and the people a person associates with.

In American society, many of the activities that have traditionally been regarded as protected from government regulation are known as private. For example, you probably know that the First Amendment to the U.S. Constitution guarantees every citizen the right to free speech. However, that does not mean that you can say anything you want whenever you want. The courts have consistently ruled that the government has the right to regulate speech that takes place in certain public areas.

Couples must apply for a marriage liscence even when married in a church or synagogue.

Likewise, Americans are free to practice whatever religion they like, but public expressions of religious sentiment can be regulated. Teachers in public schools cannot have their students pray or engage in other forms of religious worship or activity, for instance. You are free to bar anyone you like from your home, which is a sphere of private life, but a business cannot refuse to serve someone because of race or sex.

It would seem that in these regards marriage would be the most private of activities. After all, what 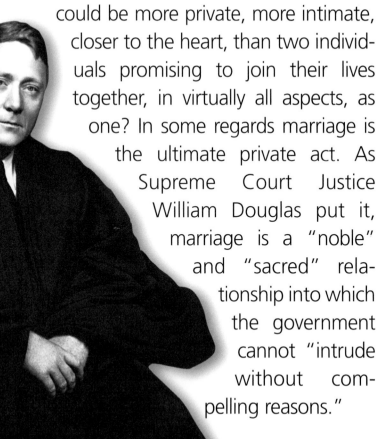 could be more private, more intimate, closer to the heart, than two individuals promising to join their lives together, in virtually all aspects, as one? In some regards marriage is the ultimate private act. As Supreme Court Justice William Douglas put it, marriage is a "noble" and "sacred" relationship into which the government cannot "intrude without compelling reasons."

Supreme Court
Justice William
Douglas

Legally speaking, it is also clear that marriage has public aspects as well. As we mentioned before, you need a license to be legally married. Public records must be kept of marriages, as they are of births and deaths. Officially dissolving a marriage also requires the involvement of the legal system. If marriage is such a private act, why should this be so?

Some History

The idea that marriage is primarily a romantic or emotional ideal is a relatively new one in Western culture. Obviously, the evolution of the idea of marriage in this culture is an extremely complicated topic, but it is accurate to say that for centuries marriage was understood to be as much an economic and legal arrangement as it was a romantic one. Religious teachings also provided marriage with a spiritual and ceremonial side, but as an institution marriage operated first and foremost as a legal arrangement to guarantee heredity and the orderly transfer of property between generations—that is, within families from parents to children.

This was especially important when the ownership of land was the primary measure of wealth. Marriage worked fundamentally as an economic arrangement, with the woman herself as an economic asset that would add to a family's wealth and financial well-being. In agreeing

CHAVEZ HIGH SCHOOL
LIBRARY
HOUSTON, TEXAS

to marry a woman, a man promised to support her economically in exchange for, essentially, her ability to bear children. Often, the marriage itself was a chance for the man to enrich himself, for a woman brought with her a dowry—a payment in money, goods, or land from her birth family to her new husband. The children she was expected to bear were also economic assets, especially in poorer families, where they served as labor. In predominantly agricultural societies, where most work was done in the fields, this was especially important. As they still are in many cultures around the globe, marriages were arranged for economic reasons as often as they were for any personal compatibility, let alone love, between the partners.

The legal institution of marriage served to ensure that the family's property would be passed on to the children. Among the ruling classes—the nobility and monarchy—marriage worked as a legal way to transfer power as well. Children from the marriages of the nobility inherited their titles, property, and political power. The children of the monarch could inherit the throne. At such levels of society, marriages were often arranged to cement political and strategic alliances. The uniting of two prominent families by marriage was a way to increase the wealth and power of both.

The end of a marriage, too, could have important political consequences. In the sixteenth century, for example, King Henry VIII of England decided he no longer wanted to be married to his wife, Catherine of Aragon, who was the daughter of King Ferdinand and Queen Isabella of Spain. Among the political consequences of this decision was England's break with the Catholic Church, its conversion to Protestantism, and more than two centuries of war with Spain and France.

All this is not to say that love and other emotions never played a role in marriage. Of course they did, to a greater or lesser degree depending on the people involved. But the institution of marriage as we know it in the United States today evolved as a public, legal arrangement as much as it did a private, romantic one.

The Public Interest Today

All right, you say, that makes sense, but things have changed a lot since then. We live in a democracy now; land ownership is no longer the primary source of wealth; kings, queens, and nobles are no longer the ruling class; and women enjoy much greater personal and economic freedom, including control over reproduction. Marriage is now generally regarded more as a personal, emotional matter than as an economic arrangement. So why should the government still have an interest in regulating marriage?

Marriage still serves as the primary way to regulate the transfer of property and wealth—inheritance—across generations. In many aspects, for example, children born outside of marriage do not have the same legal rights as children born of a marriage. Although children in the United States are no longer viewed as economic assets in the sense that they serve as labor, this change in the way children are regarded is actually a reason why marriage remains a legal and public institution rather than a private, personal, or religious arrangement.

Put simply, American society still believes that marriage is the best way to regulate family relationships, specifically the care of children, for the greatest benefit of children and society. Today, although many people argue about the best methods of doing so, few people disagree with the idea that society has a good reason to be interested in how its children are raised. Under certain circumstances, most people would agree—and the law agrees with them—the government even has the right to come between parents and their children. Abuse and neglect are examples of such situations. In the past two decades, as public awareness of child abuse and neglect has increased, the number of cases in which the courts and government agencies act to remove children from their home has risen enormously.

England broke away from the Catholic church due to King Henry VIII's divorce

In historical terms, this is a relatively new development in the United States. It is only in the last one hundred years or so that laws have been passed specifically for the protection of children. Before that, children were considered property, and the government had next to no legal right to intervene in family life, even in the interest of protecting children's well-being. As the *Oxford Companion to the Supreme Court* puts it, "families existed in a constitutionally protected private realm of society . . . There is a realm of family life that the state [i.e., the government] cannot enter without substantial justification."

The increase in awareness of the extent of child abuse and neglect comes at the end of a long period of change in social attitudes about marriage. An increasing number of Americans regard marriage as a matter of individual choice, morality, and freedom. This trend has become particularly evident since the 1960s. Today, fewer Americans are choosing to get married than at any time in this century, and more Americans are choosing to have children outside of marriage. Changes in the law have made divorce easier than ever to obtain, and the divorce rate has risen to its highest level in history.

During this same period, the level of child abuse and neglect, childhood poverty, and the rate of crime, including juvenile crime, has also risen to extremely high levels. Although the reasons for this are complex, a large part of American society blames a decreasing commitment to marriage and a decline in so-called family values. From this point of view, one of the best things society can do to protect children is to make sure that they are raised in a secure home, which many people define as one in which there are married parents. The result in many states has been a renewed emphasis on marriage as a public institution that society has an interest in encouraging and regulating. This has led to various legal incentives encouraging marriage, such as tax breaks, and proposals for laws that make it tougher to obtain divorces and that reward couples that remain married. Although many Americans do not agree that these steps represent a real solution, it is clear that marriage—and by extension, divorce—remains a public social issue as well as a private emotional one.

CHAPTER 3

Beginning the Process

Okay, Caitlin says to herself, now I know why society takes an interest in regulating marriage. But what is actually going to happen to us—my mother and father and my sister? How do they actually get the divorce? Do we all have to go to court? Will we have to stand up in court and testify? Will there be lawyers involved? Isn't it the job of lawyers to argue with each other? Does that mean that the lawyers will get Mom and Dad to be angry with each other? What is going to happen now?

The Marriage Contract

Legally, marriage is a kind of contract. Most people probably think of a contract as a business or work arrangement, but in legal terms a contract can be any agreement between two parties, whether they are individuals, businesses or corporations, or even countries. (A treaty, for example, is a kind of contract between two nations.)

The classic legal definition of a contract is a *"consideration in exchange for a promise."* In other words, a contract is an agreement to do something specific or perform a specific service in return for some reward, often a monetary payment. A well-known example of a contract is the employment agreement that an athlete signs with his or her team. A player agrees to provide a service—play basketball for the San Antonio Spurs, for example—in exchange for an agreed-upon salary. Usually quite a large one these days.

Another way of viewing a contract is as an exchange of mutual, or reciprocal, obligations or promises. It is easy to understand the idea of marriage as a contract in this way. Historically, marriage was an exchange of promises to provide certain things—economic support, sexual access and fidelity, the woman's ability to bear children and the man's ability to father them, and child raising, among others.

Failure to live up to these obligations constituted legal grounds for divorce, which can be understood in this sense as legal recognition that the contract has been broken. For example, adultery—a sexual relationship with a person other than the spouse—is sufficient

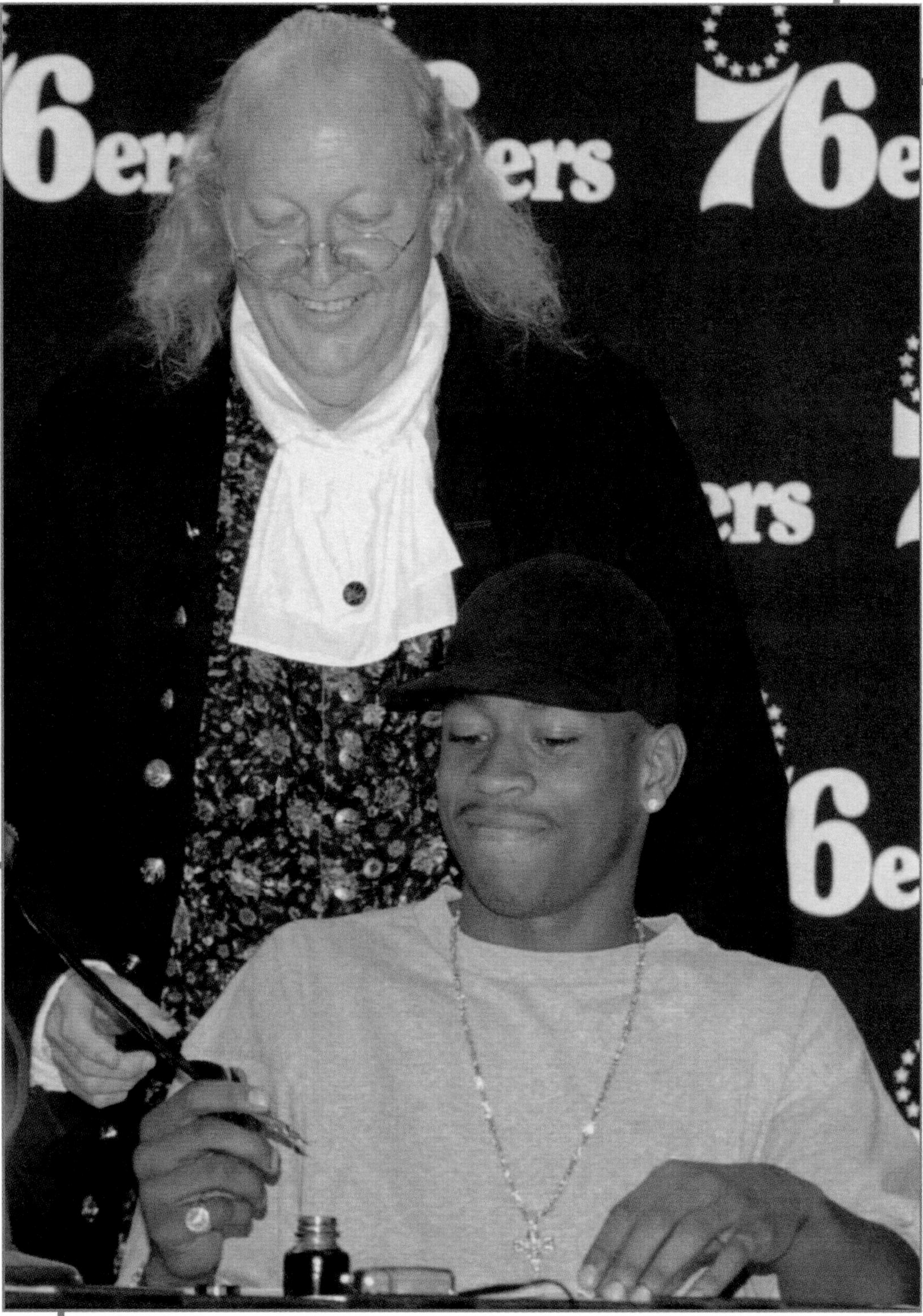
76ers
76ers
76ers

legal reason for a divorce. This means that if one spouse charges the other with adultery, and the charge can be proven in court, the marriage can be dissolved by the court even if only one spouse wants a divorce.

Likewise, what is known in legal terms as constructive abandonment is sufficient grounds for one spouse to be granted a divorce. Constructive abandonment means the persistent refusal, over a legally defined period of time, to have sexual relations with your spouse. Actual abandonment, or desertion, means that a spouse has left the marriage or home physically—that is, is living elsewhere. Desertion is also grounds for divorce. Other legal grounds for divorce include physical, verbal, or emotional abuse. Inability to have sexual relations can be grounds for divorce, as, in some jurisdictions, can be certain kinds of severe mental illness.

No Fault

You may have noticed that all these grounds for divorce have one thing in common—they assign fault to one party for *breaching*, or breaking, the terms of the marriage contract. The logic behind this is that because one party has failed to live up to his or her obligations, the other spouse is entitled to be released from the marriage contract. Because the second party did not herself

NBA players, like Allen Iverson, must sign contracts too.

break the contract, she (historically, this has most often been true of women) is still entitled to some of the benefits that the husband promised to provide. Usually this takes the form of continued financial assistance in the form of alimony and child support.

Until the last thirty years or so, these were the only grounds on which a married couple could obtain a legal divorce. In other words, at least one of them had to behave badly, in the sense of violating the marriage agreement. That a couple simply grew tired of each other, or did not want to be married anymore, without either one of them necessarily having acted poorly, was not sufficient reason for a legal divorce. In such cases, the couple's choices were limited. They could split up, but not legally. One spouse could falsely accuse the other of adultery or other grounds for divorce. Sometimes couples even agreed to make false accusations and to arrange the proof the court needed—for example, by taking a photograph of one of them in a bed with someone else. Or they could simply live with the situation and try to make the best of it.

In the 1960s, that began to change. As people began to put more emphasis on the private aspect or marriage, it became more widely accepted that a marriage could fail or end without it necessarily being anyone's fault. Over time, the law changed to allow couples to legally divorce if both spouses wanted to. This development is sometimes referred to as no-fault divorce. No reason had to be given or proven aside from incompatibility, which means basically that the couple did not or could not get along with each other anymore. The adoption of no-fault divorce laws is probably the factor most responsible for the rise in the divorce rate in the United States since the 1960s.

Still Legal

No-fault divorce makes it possible to obtain a legal divorce with the minimal involvement of the court system, and many couples do divorce this way. Little more is required than filing documents with the court and waiting a prescribed length of time for the divorce to become official.

However, just because a couple agree that they are incompatible and that they both want a divorce does not mean that they will agree on how to divorce—that is, on what the terms will be. A couple can both want to end a marriage legally and not be able to agree on such things as alimony, child custody, and division of property.

This is one more reason why divorce remains a legal matter as much as a personal one. Deciding who gets to live in the family house is often a huge issue, for example. Child care, especially, is an arrangement in which society takes a huge interest. If the parties to a divorce cannot agree on how the responsibility for taking care of their children will be arranged, the result is often neglect or abuse of the children. In such situations, society at large often ends up with the responsibility for raising such children or, in the worst-case scenario, in dealing with the consequences of abuse and neglect, including criminal behavior, substance abuse, poverty, and related issues.

Process

The legal process of divorce begins with one or both partners deciding that they want to put a legal end to their marriage. This is done by filing legal papers—known generally as a petition—with the court that has jurisdiction over divorces in that particular place. Jurisdiction is the legal authority of a court. Jurisdiction can be both physical, in the sense of a geographical area—a county, state, etc.—or over a specific area of law, such as criminal law. Most divorces are handled in the civil part of a state's court system. Civil court deals with legal matters other than the commission of crimes.

If both parties want a divorce and agree on the terms, then the divorce is said to be uncontested. In this case, no hearings or court appearances are necessary in most states. After a short waiting period to allow the parties to change their minds, the divorce becomes official. The parties are now legally divorced, and both are free to marry again if they want to. The divorce agreement specifies the terms of such matters as division of property, alimony, and child custody. The divorce settlement then becomes legally binding on both parties, with both obligated to fulfill their side of the deal.

Once again, it is important to remember that divorce is only the legal end of a marriage. From the perspective of American society, the couple are divorced, but certain religions, for example, do not accept divorce. The Roman Catholic Church, for instance, to which more than 60 million Americans belong, does not allow divorce. There is nothing to prevent a Roman Catholic couple from obtaining a legal divorce, but in the eyes of the church the couple are still married, and neither partner is free to remarry in the church. In some predominantly Roman Catholic countries, legal divorce may be difficult or even impossible to obtain. The Republic of Ireland, for example, does not allow divorce.

In the Republic of Ireland, divorce is not allowed.

If the couple cannot agree on the terms of the divorce or the settlement, the divorce is said to be contested. In these circumstances, the divorce will be heard as a case in court, before a judge, who either works to bring the couple to an agreement or imposes one on them.

In 1994, which is the most recent year for which comprehensive statistics are available, slightly more than 2.3 million marriages were performed in the United States. That same year, there were almost 1.2 million divorces. No reliable statistics are available for how many of those divorces were settled amicably between the parties or how many were settled in court.

Some states offer alternatives to a no-fault or uncontested divorce and a full-blown legal hearing. In some jurisdictions, divorcing couples can tell their stories to mediators or arbiters. These are trained, impartial listeners who work with a divorcing couple to bring about a settlement that they both can live with. The goal of mediation is to resolve the case without a court hearing, which can be both emotionally damaging and extremely expensive.

Lawyers

What makes a divorce case so expensive are lawyers. A lawyer is a professional who has been trained in the law. He or she has successfully completed a minimum of three years of specialized training at a law school after obtaining an undergraduate college degree. He or she then must pass a standardized licensing examination and receive the approval of a professional licensing board in the jurisdiction where he or she wishes to practice. Some lawyers specialize in the practice of divorce law. Like most lawyers, they tend to be very well paid for their training and expertise. In a long, drawn-out court case that requires a lot of time in court, a lawyer's fee can run to the tens and even hundreds of thousands of dollars. On average, child-custody disputes alone take one to three years to settle and cost anywhere from $50,000 to $300,000.

Are lawyers absolutely required in a divorce case? Strictly speaking, no. Obviously, one of the attractions of the no-fault or so-called do-it-yourself type of divorce is that it enables the parties to avoid the expense of lawyers' fees. Although there are few reliable statistics on how many divorces are settled in this way, the number has risen consistently through the past decade.

Even if a couple do decide that their divorce case needs to be heard by a court, there is no law that requires either of them to hire a lawyer. Like the parties in any kind of case in the legal system, the parties to a divorce have the right to represent themselves in court if they wish to, although a responsible judge will probably discourage them from doing so. Most people are simply not sufficiently knowledgeable about the complexities of the law to represent themselves competently in a court-room, and a divorce hearing is no place to begin learning. Representing yourself can put you at a severe legal disadvantage, particularly if the other party has a lawyer. It is significant that lawyers almost never represent themselves, even though, obviously, they are proficient in the law. In fact, lawyers have a famous saying about representing themselves: "A lawyer who represents himself or herself has a fool for a client."

The role that lawyers play in divorce is controversial. Some people believe that lawyers encourage a confrontational, win-at-all-costs attitude in the parties to a divorce. Fairly or unfairly, lawyers are sometimes accused of intentionally prolonging or increasing the conflict in a divorce case in order to increase their own fees. Divorce lawyers usually charge by the number of hours they spend on a case; in general, the longer the case drags on, the more they are paid. There have certainly been cases in which a divorcing couple spend huge amounts of time in court arguing over the division of property, for example, only to find at the end of the case that the largest amount of that property essentially goes to their lawyers in fees.

Hiring a lawyer does not necessarily mean that the case will become needlessly expensive or destructive, however. Many divorce lawyers are competent and ethical, of course, and genuinely have the best interests of their clients at heart. If one party to the divorce hires a lawyer, the other should almost certainly have one. Even if the case does not wind up in court, some people find lawyers helpful in guiding them through the process. If there is going to be a dispute about property or custody, it is important to make sure to get the best advice possible. In most circumstances, that means hiring a lawyer.

However, the best outcome of all, when possible, is for both parties to work out a settlement on their own, outside of court, that is fair to both of them. In doing so, a divorcing couple avoid needless expense and inflicting additional emotional damage on each other and other family members. An ethical divorce attorney will advise them to do so and will be a help rather than a hindrance in bringing this about.

CHAPTER 4

In Court

So what happens if a divorce case does wind up in court? If the couple cannot reach an agreement and they hire lawyers? What actually happens in divorce court?

First of all, the term divorce court is not strictly accurate. In many states and jurisdictions, the courts where divorces are heard are not actually named divorce court. In New York State, for example, divorces are heard in the civil portion of Superior Court. Even so, many people commonly use the term divorce court to refer generally to the courts where divorce hearings are held.

The Hearing

There are no trials in divorce court. No one is found guilty of committing a crime or liable for a civil infringement of the law. The court's job in a divorce case is not to find one party right or wrong but to determine what are the fairest terms under which a couple may end their marriage. The court must consider more than just the best interests of the couple; there may be children involved, and the court also considers the interests of society.

There are no juries in divorce court. The case is both presided over and heard by a judge, who renders a decision at the end if the couple have been unable to reach an agreement by that point. The vast majority of divorce cases are settled before the judge has to render a decision. This means that the couple, with the help of their lawyers, reach an agreement at some point before the judge makes a decision. For many divorcing couples, the prospect of having their case actually heard in front of a judge spurs them to reach a settlement.

A divorce case in court is conducted in the form of hearings. A hearing is less formal than a trial and is governed by fewer rules of procedure. Basically, a hearing is an opportunity to present arguments before a judge.

In a divorce hearing, both sides present their arguments, usually through their lawyer or lawyers. They present evidence, either through their own testimony or those of witnesses, about the marriage and why they are seeking a divorce. Lawyers for the other party then have the right to cross-examine these witnesses. In general, the rules of evidence for a hearing are much less strict than they would be for a trial. Judges have considerable discretion about what kind of testimony they will allow and how much credence they will give to it.

These days, a judge is unlikely to deny a divorce to a couple even if one party is opposed to it. For the most part, the most intense legal and emotional conflict in a divorce case occurs over the terms of the divorce—specifically, over the division of property and child custody. Property and child-custody arguments are generally heard in separate hearings.

Alimony and Property

In a property hearing, the judge hears testimony about the financial status and lifestyle of the couple during their marriage. Evidence about each partner's level of education, employment history, and income is usually presented. Often the parties present testimony about their understanding of the marriage's financial arrangement. For example, if the wife agreed to halt her own education and career in order to help put her husband through medical school and raise their children, her prospects for resuming her career after the divorce may be limited. The judge would almost certainly consider these facts in making his or her decision.

Today more married women work than at any previous time in American history. This means that more married women are likely to have their own income during a marriage and that their economic contribution to a marriage may be easier for a judge to quantify in determining questions of property and financial support.

This is a relatively new development, however. Traditionally, the most common arrangement featured a husband who worked and a wife who maintained the home and raised children. In such circumstances, it was generally assumed that the wife in a divorce was entitled to some portion of her former spouse's income as support for herself after the divorce.

Today this may or may not be true. In general, divorce court judges are more likely than in the past to expect a woman to be responsible for her own financial support after the divorce. Even so, a judge weighs the overall contribution made by the woman to the

These days, a judge is unlikely to deny a divorce even if one party is opposed to it.

couple's lifestyle. In general, the woman is still held to be entitled to some expectation of a comparable life-style after the divorce, for which the court makes the husband responsible in the form of alimony.

The presumption that a woman is entitled to some degree of alimony or support reflects the traditional legal view of marriage as a contract or agreement in which the woman's capacity to bear children and her home-making skills were regarded as the chief asset she brought to a marriage, in exchange for which she was entitled to financial support. Although attitudes are changing, society and the law still regard a woman as entitled to some level of financial support after the divorce, particularly if the marriage is ended through no fault of hers.

If her husband was physically abusive, for example, the law does not expect a woman to choose between tolerating such abuse or relinquishing a substantial degree of the financial support she was entitled to during the marriage. In theory, at least, the law does not expect a partner who lives up to his or her side of the marriage agreement to suffer financially because the misconduct of the other makes a divorce desirable or necessary.

Even so, the majority of women experience a reduction in lifestyle, measured strictly economically, after a divorce. Overall, divorce is a major cause of women's impoverishment. The most comprehensive study of this issue was done in the late 1980s. It indicated that on average, a woman's spending money declined by 73 percent after a divorce. By contrast, a man's spending money increased by 42 percent.

In most jurisdictions, a judge may, after hearing arguments from both sides, establish whatever alimony or support payments he or she finds fair. The judge in a divorce case has enormous discretion over such arrangements. He or she may order alimony as a permanent arrangement that can be changed only by petitioning the court and demonstrating that the financial circumstances of either partner has changed. Alimony may be a temporary arrangement—for example, a judge may order the husband to pay support for a specific period of time. The judge may require the husband to pay alimony for as long as it takes the wife to educate herself so that she can support herself financially.

The form of alimony can vary. Often, alimony is set at a certain amount to be paid each month, but in some cases the parties may agree to a one-time lump sum payment. In all cases, alimony ends when a woman remarries.

Although it does not happen often, women sometimes pay men alimony after a divorce. This has become more common as more and more women make independent careers for themselves and as a growing number of men stay at home to raise children while their wives work—the so-called Mr. Mom or house-husband scenario. Even if there are no children involved, if the man can demonstrate that he expected a certain level of financial support from his wife as a condition of agreeing to marry and that the marriage is ending through no fault of his own, he is entitled to some level of financial support or alimony. However, traditional social attitudes play a role here, too. Because men have traditionally been expected to be more independent financially than women, it can still be hard for a man to convince a court that he should receive alimony.

In most states, the woman is also entitled to some share of whatever property the couple has accumulated during the marriage, regardless of whether she has worked or not. Some states have what are called community-property laws, which mandate that all property acquired during the marriage be split equally between the divorcing partners.

In theory, this seems like an exceedingly fair arrangement, but it can be difficult to carry out in practice. For example, suppose the chief property that a married couple have accumulated together is a house. How can a house be split equally between two people? There have been cases, where the house was big enough and

More and more men are becoming Mr. Moms, while their wives go to work

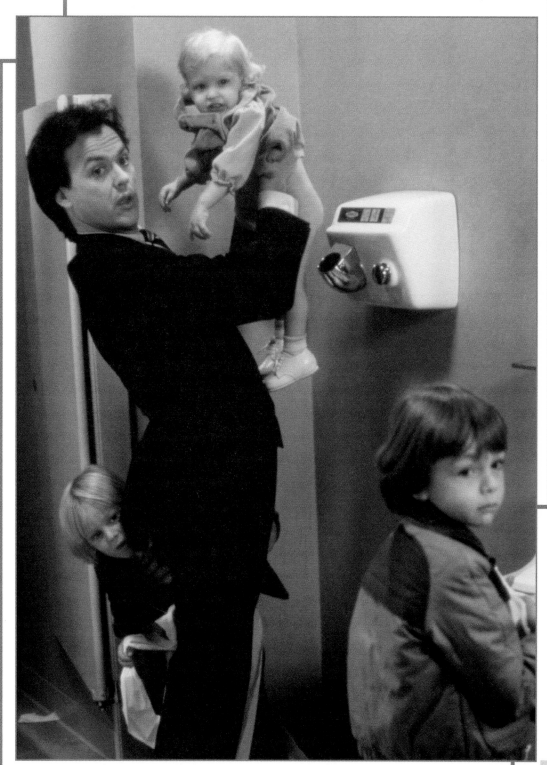

neither party would relinquish claim to it, of a judge ordering the couple to share the house—by living in separate wings, for example. A more likely scenario is that the judge orders the couple to sell the house and divide the proceeds between them. Or the judge might try to persuade the two to agree to an arrangement whereby one party buys the other's share in the house.

You can easily see how alimony and property settlements offer opportunities for disagreement that would try the patience of even the wisest judge. There is virtually no limit to the kinds of things that divorcing couples argue about in property settlements—everything from a house to pets to family heirlooms to the wedding gifts to season tickets at the nearest stadium. When couples cannot agree on how such things should be divided, it becomes the responsibility of the court, after hearings, to decide for them.

Child Custody

Child custody is often the stormiest issue of a divorce hearing. Essentially, child custody means which parent the child or children will live with after the divorce. The parent assigned physical custody also most often has what is called legal custody—the right and responsibility to make the primary decisions regarding the child. The parent with custody thus has the primary responsibility for the day-today care and raising of the child, often with financial assistance—child support—from the noncustodial parent. Again, if the couple cannot agree, the judge will determine the level of child support after a hearing. Child support is separate from alimony and is to be used only for the expenses of the divorcing couple's children, including food, clothing, housing, medical expenses, and education.

The judge essentially has two options in making a decision following a custody hearing: to award custody to either the mother or the father. For many years, until recently, there was what was known as the maternal presumption or maternal preference in determining custody. That meant that in the absence of evidence to the contrary—for example, that the mother was abusive or neglectful—it was assumed that the children were best off in her custody. In such cases, the court would assign the father visitation rights—specified time that he could spend with his children. Most often, this was every other weekend. Such arrangements once again reflected the assumption that the standard or best arrangement of family life featured a father who worked and a mother who kept the home and raised the children, as well as the belief that the mother-child relationship was the most important one for the child's healthy development and well-being.

Today this kind of arrangement is not nearly as common as it once was. Even so, the maternal presumption is still the standard most often used in determining custody, and the most common arrangement has the mother with custody and the father paying child support and exercising "reasonable visitation" rights. For the past thirty years, this has been the outcome in approximately 85 percent of custody cases.

In recent years, there has been an increase in the number of fathers who are awarded custody. This can be seen as society's and the law's recognition of the importance of the father in the life of a child, although some women's groups disagree. Instead, they see this trend toward paternal custody as reflecting a backlash against the changes in society that have allowed women greater independence and economic opportunity. As an example, they point to the growing number of cases in which fathers have successfully argued that their former wife's devotion to her career made her a less than adequate mother. They argue that such women are being punished for pursuing a career in the same way that men have traditionally been expected to. Some men respond that the maternal presumption standard penalizes men in the same way.

Criteria

So what standards does the judge use in determining which parent should receive custody? The traditional standard, and by far still the most common, is called the best interests standard. Put simply, the judge is supposed to award custody based on what would be in the best interests of the child. At the custody hearing, therefore, the judge hears and weighs evidence indicating whether the child would be better off, in terms of his or her overall well-being, with the father or with the mother. Such testimony may be provided by the parents themselves, by friends and other family members with insight into the family situation, and by expert witnesses, such as psychologists, social workers, teachers, and family counselors. In general, however, a father in such a hearing has to present evidence to overcome the maternal presumption that the children are better off in the custody of their mother.

Until recently, the best interests standard was the law in all fifty states. In recent years, a few states, including Minnesota, Washington, and West Virginia, have been using a different standard, which is known generally as the primary caretaker preference. This standard holds that custody should be awarded to the parent who has spent the most time during the marriage engaging in the primary child-care duties. These are defined as planning meals, bathing and dressing the child, purchasing clothes, obtaining medical care, arranging for child care, putting the child to bed, disciplining the child, and teaching basic educational skills, such as reading and writing.

Joint Custody

Another custody option is available for families that are divorcing. Since 1979, virtually all fifty states have allowed a divorcing couple to establish joint custody of their kids. Joint custody is basically just what it says: An agreement by the parents to share the decision-making responsibility for their children as well as physical custody of them. The details of the arrangement can be as specific or as informal as the parents want them to be. In practice, the actual living arrangements that families establish under a joint custody arrangement vary greatly.

Parents interested in having joint custody must reach an agreement that they wish to share custody of their children; a judge cannot impose joint custody on them. Joint custody has become an increasingly popular alternative. In California, where the first joint custody law was passed in 1979, studies have indicated that joint custody is used by 75 to 90 percent of divorcing couples.

CHAPTER 5

So What's It to You?

By now Caitlin and Allison know more than they ever thought they would about divorce and the court system. The strange thing is that it doesn't seem as if any of it has much to do with them. All of it is about their parents, which they can understand, but it still leaves them wondering what role they will play in the legal process?

Just as children cannot really influence their parents' decision to divorce, they generally play a very small role in the legal process that brings the marriage to an end. For the most part, children, particularly small children, are not called upon to testify in court about their parents' marriage. Even when they are the focus of custody hearings, children generally are not given the opportunity to testify.

Until very recently, the child's own wishes were not a factor that a judge needed to consider when determining custody. Often the court determined what was in the best interests of the child without ever hearing directly from the child itself. If the child's thoughts on the matter were heard in any way by the court, it was usually indirectly, most often through the testimony of psychologists, counselors, or social workers who interviewed the child.

In recent years, older children have been given a much greater opportunity to be heard in court about child-care arrangements after the divorce. Many states now allow children older than fourteen to express their thoughts or state a preference at a hearing, which the judge can then consider as a factor in making a decision. Some states even allow children younger than fourteen to be heard, if the judge thinks that such testimony will be helpful. However, in most cases the judge still has enormous discretion as to whether the child will be heard at all.

You should remember that it is not necessarily a good thing to have the opportunity to testify in court. In all likelihood, the child of parents who are divorcing feels a tremendous range of emotions about both of them, including a great deal of love for both. Divorce can be difficult enough emotionally already; to be put in a position of having to choose publicly between parents can be devastating. Nevertheless, if older children do have a preference they wish to express, an increasing number of courts allow them this opportunity.

There is generally no legal reason why a child cannot attend his or her parents' divorce hearings, but why would you want to? How much do you enjoy hearing your parents argue at home, if they do? Do you like to hear your father tell your mother all the ways in which she has been inadequate as a wife or a parent, or vice versa? Do you enjoy hearing your parents argue at home about money? Do you like it when your parents criticize each other? Odds are that you will not enjoy hearing these arguments continued in court either.

So if the children of divorcing parents have so little power to affect the legal process, why is it so important that they know about it? There are many reasons, but perhaps the most important is a simple one: If your parents are divorcing, the outcome of that legal process will greatly affect your life. A lot about divorce is scary, both for parents and their children. The most frightening thing about divorce might be that it represents a giant step into the unknown for the entire family. Learning all you can about the legal process of divorce is one way to reduce that element of the unknown.

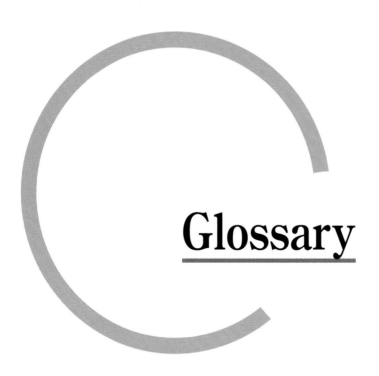

Glossary

abandonment The act of leaving a marriage informally or outside the legal system.

alimony Payment made to a spouse after divorce.

breach To break or fail to live up to the terms of a contract, promise, or agreement.

child support Payment made by a parent after a divorce for the care and education of the children of the marriage.

consideration Something given, such as a payment, in exchange for goods or a service.

contract In legal terms, an agreement to provide goods or a service in exchange for financial compensation or some other consideration.

custody Immediate responsibility for the care of a child.

divorce   The legal termination of a marriage.

hearing   Legal proceeding, less formal than a trial, in which evidence and/or arguments are presented before a judge for a decision.

jurisdiction   The legal authority of a court of law.

legal custody   In a divorce case, the legal responsibility for raising a child assigned by a court.

maternal presumption   The belief, often cited in child-custody matters, that a child is always better off with his or her mother than with his or her father.

prenuptial agreement   An agreement made by a couple before marriage that outlines the financial and other terms that will apply if the marriage ends in divorce.

primary caretaker   The parent, family member, or other person who actually performs most of the day-to-day tasks involved in raising a child.

private   In legal terms, that which concerns matters of personal behavior. Under U.S. law in general, the government has a lesser right to control private activity than it does public activity.

promise   In legal terms, an agreement to provide goods or a service.

Where to Go for Help

Children's Defense Fund

25 E Street NW
Washington, DC 20001
(202) 628-8787

e-mail: cdfinfo@childrensdefense.org (or go to their
Web site for regional offices: http://www.childrens-
defense.org/contacts.html)

Children's Rights Council

300 I Street NE, Suite 401
Washington, DC 20002
(202) 547-6227

NEO Teenline

A confidential, judgment-free hotline where teens
can discuss their problems with caring listeners. Call

1(800) 272-TEEN (8336) in the United States or Canada.

Web Sites

The Kids' Corner

http://eros.the park.com/volunteer/safehaven/divorce/divorce_kids.htm

For kids whose families are going through or have been through a divorce, with links to sites specifically for teens and sites in Canada.

The Kids' Page at Successful Steps

http://www.positivesteps.com/Kids.htm

Lots of information and support for kids about step-families, parents, siblings, abandonment, and other subjects.

My Two Homes

http://www.mytwohomes.com/

A site where kids can order cool stuff to make life with two homes easier: a calendar to keep track of days with Mom and days with Dad, a handbook, a photo album, and more.

For Further Reading

American Bar Association Family Law Section. *My Parents Are Getting Divorced: A Handbook for Kids (Family Advocate).* Chicago: American Bar Association, 1996.

Ayers, William. *A Kind and Just Parent: The Children of Juvenile Court.* Boston: Beacon, 1997.

Feld, Barry C. *Bad Kids: Race and the Transformation of Juvenile Court.* New York: Oxford, 1999.

Goldstein, Joseph, Albert J. Solnit, Sonja Goldstein, and Anna Freud. *The Best Interests of the Child: The Least Detrimental Alternative.* New York: Free Press, 1998.

Hawes, Joseph M. *The Children's Rights Movement in the United States: A History of Advocacy and Protection.* Boston: Twayne, 1991.

Hubner, John, and Jill Wolfson. *Somebody Else's Children: The Courts, the Kids, and the Struggle to Save America's Troubled Children.* New York: Three Rivers, 1996.

Humes, Edward. *No Matter How Loud I Shout: A Year in the Life of Juvenile Court.* New York: Touchstone, 1996.

Mayle, Peter. *Why Are We Getting a Divorce?* New York: Harmony Books, 1988.

Nightingale, Lois V. *My Parents Still Love Me Even Though They're Getting Divorced (an interactive tale for children).* Yorba Linda, CA: Nightingale Rose Publications, 1997.

U.S. Department of Health and Human Services. *Trends in the Well-Being of America's Children and Youth 1998.* Washington: U.S. Government Printing Office, 1999.

Vito, Gennaro F., Richard Tewksbury, and Deborah G. Wilson. *The Juvenile Justice System: Concepts and Issues.* Prospect Heights, IL: Waveland Press, 1999.

Index

About the Author

Anne Bianchi is an attorney in Westchester County, New York. She has written several books on legal issues for young adults

Photo Credits

Cover and pp. 13, 16 by Kristen Artz; p.4 © Archive Photos; p.19 © International Stock; pp. 8, 30 © AP Photo; pp. 20, 24, 35 © Corbis; p.43 © Uniphoto; p.47 © The Everett Collection.

Design and Layout

Michael J. Caroleo

Series Editor

Erica Smith